4TH GRADE HISTORY BOOK MAYANS AND INCAS OF SOUTH AMERICA

Speedy Publishing LLC
40 E. Main St. #1156
Newark, DE 19711
www.speedypublishing.com

Copyright 2018

All Rights reserved. No part of this book may be reproduced or used in any way or form or by any means whether electronic or mechanical, this means that you cannot record or photocopy any material ideas or tips that are provided in this book.

The two most dominant and advanced civilizations that developed in the Americas were the Maya, and the Inca.

MAYA CIVILIZATION

The Ancient Mayan lived in the Yucatán around 2600 B.C. Today, this area is southern Mexico, Guatemala, northern Belize and western Honduras.

The position of king was usually inherited by the oldest son. If there wasn't a son then the oldest brother became king.

NO HAY PASO

The Maya considered crossed eyes, flat foreheads, and big noses to be beautiful features. They would use makeup to try and make their noses appear large.

VIVA
EL PERU

INCA EMPIRE

The Inca Empire existed in Peru. The Empire had ruled much of the region since the early 1400s.

The Inca Empire had large stone cities, beautiful temples, an advanced government, a detailed tax system, and a road system.

Many people had to pay their taxes through labor. They worked for the government as soldiers, builders, or farmers in order to pay their taxes.

www.ingramcontent.com/pod-product-compliance
Lightning Source LLC
Chambersburg PA
CBHW081243130726

47997CB00009B/2981